DIRT

DIRT

poems by
Jo McDougall

AUTUMN HOUSE PRESS · PITTSBURGH

Text and cover design: Kathy Boykowycz
Consulting editor: Eva Maria Simms

Printed in the U.S.A.
ISBN: 0-9669419-3-4
Library of Congress Control Number: 2001 132054

In memory of Charla, my daughter
and
for Duke, my son

ACKNOWLEDGEMENTS

Grateful acknowledgement is made to the editors of the following publications in which these poems, some in different versions, have appeared: *Women Who Marry Houses*, a chapbook published by Coyote Love Press; *The Arkansas Literary Forum*, *Arkansas Times*, *Controlled Burn*, *The Little Balkans Review*, *New Letters*, *New Orleans Review*, *Paragraph*, *Slow Dancer*.

Thanks to the editors of *The Hudson Review* in which "Threads" first appeared (Spring 2000, Vol. LIII, No. 1) and to the editors of *The Kenyon Review* in which "What We Need" first appeared (*The Kenyon Review*—New Series, Spring 1999, Vol. XXI, No. 2).

"For Stephen, Who Owns a Bag of My Cut Fingernails Carried in the Mouth of an Eel Who Swam the Caddo" was included in *Towns Facing Railroads*, a multi-media performance piece staged May, 1993, at Pittsburg State University, Pittsburg, Kansas; John Green, director.

The following poems provide partial text for *A Very Fine House*, a collaborative installation project with artist Ann deVere: "Smoke," "Having Just Met," "Mockingbird," "Scorch" (as "Ribbon"), "Kansas Town When the Sun Goes Down," "A Good Woman," "On the Brink" (as "Luck"), "A Second Cup of Coffee" (as "Wheresoever"), "Standing at a New Grave," "How to Imagine How It Will Be When the Doctor Comes Out to Say," "Intersection," "Threads" (first published in *The Hudson Review*, Spring 2000, Vol. LIII, No. 1).

"Boyfriend" and "Smoke" provide partial script for *Emerson County Shaping Dream*, an independent film directed by Don Maxwell.

Publication of this book was made possible by a grant from the Pennsylvania Council on the Arts.

My thanks go to The MacDowell Colony for residencies providing me time to shape this book and to the DeWitt Wallace/ Reader's Digest foundation for funding one of those residencies.

My appreciation goes to the following for their close reading, input, and support: Miller and Jordan Williams, Sam Hazo, Donald Hall, Steve and Ann Meats, Jeanie and Tom Wilson, Jay White, Susan David, Dave and Barbara Stafford, Susan Taylor, Phillip McMath. I thank especially my husband, Charles, for his honest criticism, practical support, and never-ending encouragement.

AUTUMN HOUSE POETRY SERIES

Michael Simms, editor

OneOnOne by Jack Myers

Snow White Horses, Selected Poems 1972-1988 by Ed Ochester

The Leaving, New and Selected Poems by Sue Ellen Thompson

Dirt by Jo McDougall

CONTENTS

I

MOCKINGBIRD

I sleep in my daughter's house.
The yard bristles with moonlight.
A mockingbird sings,
notes falling at the foot of a tree.

My daughter sleeps,
dreaming the voices of children
under her lids.
Her husband, a farmer, sleeps,
dreaming his fields.

I have nothing to bring to dreams.
The mockingbird and I are happy,
losing everything.

TELLING TIME

My son and I walk away
from his sister's day-old grave.
Our backs to the sun,
the forward pitch of our shadows
tells us the time.
By sweetest accident
he inclines
his shadow, touching mine.

DIRT

Its arrogance will break your heart.
Two weeks ago
we had to coax it
into taking her body.
Today,
after a light rain,
I see it hasn't bothered
to conceal its seams.

AT A DAUGHTER'S GRAVE

It is Spring.
I hope the man planting in the next field
will stay close as he can to her
all day,
the tractor humming,
the diesel smoke
a constantly changing veil.

WHY I GET UP EACH DAY

Tomorrow, maybe, or today
sunlight will discover one red leaf.
The sound will shatter crystal.

CROSSING

One night, crossing a field,
I stepped through a skin of moonlight
like the one
found sometimes on milk.

I don't truck with moonlight anymore.
I sleep with the light on.
I've come to my senses.

STANDING AT A NEW GRAVE

In the midst of grief
the train,
wart-ugly, heartless as a toad.
I would like to shout my gratitude
as it crosses Old Cemetery Road
like a shock of rain,
blustering and insufferable and clean.

HOUSTON

I have brought her here
too late.
The cancer has advanced.
There is nothing, the doctors tell us,
they can do.

As we drive back to our motel,
hundreds of grackles
in the ornamental trees
reel out their steely, flexible song
like the paper tongues of noise-makers we used to buy
for New Year's Eve.

METAPHOR

After the coffin lid closes
over the body,
the silence
is sometimes described as noise.
It is not.
It is silence
and the mourners float upon it
like bathtub toys.

INDULGENCES

The bracelets were 14 karat,
a matched pair.
She bought them in Savannah
and wore them every day,
one on each wrist.

One summer she sold them
to pay back rent.

She remembers their every dent,
the light waffling over them,
the delicate guard chains swinging
as she walked.

Waiting for the dealer in New Orleans
to name a price,
she saw hundreds of pairs of gold bracelets,
some so small
she imagined them worn by blond children
playing on clipped lawns,
their parents smiling, looking on
as the children worried the chains to breaking
with their teeth.

GLITTERING

Some I consider wise
tell me
grief is best endured
when its edges fade,
when numbness follows disaster,
when you find
whatever safe house
time, in due time, will offer.

Once I might have agreed.
But I lost her.

Now I pray for torment,
that her glittering shapes
burn through my skin
to bone,
the wound a shifting pattern
that will not heal.

THIS MORNING

As I drive into town
the driver in front of me
runs a stop sign.
A pedestrian pulls down his cap.
A man comes out of his house
to sweep the steps.
Ordinariness
bright as raspberries.

I turn on the radio.
Somebody tells me
the day is sunny and warm.
A woman laughs

and my daughter steps out of the radio.
Grief spreads in my throat like strep.
I had forgotten, I was happy, I maybe
was humming "You Are My Lucky Star,"
a song I may have invented.
Sometimes a red geranium, a dog,
a stone
will carry me away.
But not for long.
Some memory or another of her
catches up with me and stands
like an old nun behind a desk,
ruler in hand.

KANSAS IN WINTER

The only thing alive in this landscape
is a woman filling her car with gas
at a 7-11,
unaware how important this drama is
against the farmhouses, their squares of glass dumb
against a sky empty of birds.

WEIGHT

We are watching a PeeWee game.
My husband scrambles out of the bleachers
to get a Coke.
The space beside me where he had been
grows darker in the cooling dark.
When he returns,
the plank sags slightly
with his weight.
I want to sing.

SUMMER

Every summer when I was a child,
I visited my grandmother's farm.
We didn't say much to each other,
listening to voices:
the far bark of a dog,
from somewhere, thunder,
the easy complaint
of the porch swing.

When it rains,
quickening old ashes in the fireplace,
I want to go back,
to the house that was,
the people that were,
the chores, the horses, the cat.

But what if I could?
What if someone,
glancing up from a sewing machine or a plow,
should see me there?

PIANO

It was a Steinway baby grand,
clearly beyond our means.
I think when my mother sat down to play,
plunking down and picking up each note
as if it were concrete,
she was filling the corners
of that hardscrabble house she grew up in,
revising rooms with no music
not even a radio,
where, except for an occasional sparrow,
noon lay quiet as midnight.

GROWING UP IN A SMALL TOWN

Our fathers
kept the sky
from falling.
Our mothers,
talking of recipes and funerals
and that Hopkins girl,
wove our world.

NORTH OF CABOT

I think of my grandfather's rock-bitten farm,
crops burned to dust,
crows scolding him
from the barn.
Every time he took me to the baby's grave,
he spoke of the diphtheria.
Your grandmother never got over it, he said.
Too far from town
for any doctor.

AN OLD WOMAN RECALLS
A SEA CHANGE

When I was six, she said,
every day was summer.
When I was seven, she said,
I stood at my mother's new-dug grave.
That night
I made supper for my father.
I swept each room.
I waited for him to speak.

IN 1942

We had an enemy and a war
and neighborhoods that knew our names
and fathers smiling at us
from places found only on maps.

Once in a great while,
a package would come,
a jacket or a robe embroidered with a dragon
that nobody would let us wear.

FOR STEPHEN, WHO OWNS A BAG OF MY CUT FINGERNAILS CARRIED IN THE MOUTH OF AN EEL WHO SWAM THE CADDO

On out fifteen miles past Wabbaseka,
past Seaton, Gethsemane, and Plain,
he and I grew up neighbors in houses
facing Danner's Bayou. White plantation houses,
splendid except for needing paint.

Except for occasional killings,
times were quiet.
One night the police broke into Mama Laura's place,
the Dew-Drop Inn on 3rd where the black people went.
They found where a fire had been, and bones.
She got the bones, they said, out of graves.
Then my grandfather told me about Vera,
who worked for my mother. He said that's where
they all learned.

We went to her place and hollered till she came out,
scraping the wash-house door.
We begged her to tell us. She told us no.
She said my mama would run her off,
and we were babies.
We were ten and twelve. We loved the way she
smelled.
We wanted to know about the bones.
She said we were evil children.
She said to come back in an hour.

All through high school he and I met at the bayou,
early, before flies.
We tried to do what she'd taught us. We got scared.
One April morning in my senior year,
the moon in its last quarter,
we got it. Except neither of us knew the woman
we made appear.
We scraped the twigs together
and watched them burn.

I knew we had the power.
I said we ought to tell Vera,
who'd quit us and gone home.
She died in middle August, during drought.
Neighbors who went in for the body
found in the top of her closet
a little coffin
not much bigger than a shoebox,
with owls' feet and a few thin sticks.

He went to college in Missouri.
I buried Mama and went to work for the bank.
I wrote him drought was ruining Danner's Bayou.

We never got married. It seemed as though we would.
One day I came to be in St. Louis.
Gazing in a storefront, I saw his reflection
in back of mine.
No accident, he said. He caused it.

We often used the power after that.
That time we met in Bonn, that was my doing.
That time in Platte, as the traffic light changed.

It's two years since I saw him last.
Crossing a street in Memphis,
I enter a bar in Portland, Maine.
He is nowhere around.
I freeze to think what's happening in that bayou,
the three sticks crossing,
the owl dropping a stone where the sticks cross.
The awful joy of it. The tooth, the nail, the blazing.
Looking for him, I circle through the bar.
I look in a mirror.
The person I see does not have my face,
and backs away.

KANSAS TOWN WHEN THE SUN GOES DOWN

Nebraska
hums on the horizon.

PARLORS

We were the nieces, the daughters.
They were the uncles, the fathers. They
had keys
to houses, wives, offices,
to God.
After supper they jostled into the parlor
to smoke.
They lowered their voices
away from us.
They told us
part of the joke,
some of the story.

AMERICA

They said America would be
and it was:
the people, the parks,
the wars.

My mother and my father
said their life together would be
and it was:
the farm, the dog,
the dining table.

When I was five,
during the Great Depression,
there came in the mail one day
instructions for making a stand-up paper pig.
You started with an envelope.
The back of the pig
was one of the envelope's folds.

The envelope my mother brought me
seemed endless,
vast as a field of new snow.
I made the pig.

A WOMAN REMEMBERS A NIGHT

My husband turned off the headlights of the car
as we drove a deserted road one night,
the moon as large as the Sahara.

He was Rhett, escorting Scarlett,
both of us about to take
Atlanta, our house rich with silver
and spiral stairs.

He was a tenant farmer, working shares.
I cleaned for the landlord's wife.
As we drove up to the house,
chickens flew from the porch.

BOYFRIEND

We were both in high school, sixteen,
me headed for college.
They said he was bad.
They said his dad
was the one had bitten off the sheriff's ear
the night the sheriff came looking
for the still.

I'd hang around the gym
after the football team finished its practice,
hoping to see him.
I lied to my mother.

I saw a brightness, saw us dancing,
saw children who had his eyes.
Even now, I can smell the woodsmoke
in his jacket.

He never got out of the twelfth grade.
They said he went to work for the highway.
The girl he got pregnant was thirteen.
She wasn't from here.

HETT MAYHEW EXPLAINS WHY BELTON HARRIS
KEEPS HIS SISTER GLADYS INSIDE

Oftentimes they never know, Hett says.
It's likely Gladys never suspected
and couldn't understand what the fuss was
when the family found out
about the ears, the tail, the conversion
to three toes.

Hett says when a soul's possessed
a mirror breaks.
The soul becomes the soul of a beast
and the body starts to shape itself around it.
The shattered mirror can't show
how the hair grows to cover the face.

There are, however, clues:
Trees in the yard drop their leaves
out of season.
A shovel moves.
All the doors in the house
slam shut at noon.

Hett says you may notice that
and the cats with no tails
that come to your house on Tuesdays.
Or you may not.

Hett believes
Gladys Harris never noticed
and doesn't understand why she can't go out,
why somebody burned her shoes,
why a woman near the tracks in Pine Bluff
makes all her clothes.

A GOOD WOMAN

Some days all day she said nothing to us,
going early with her Bible to bed.
She was what they called
a good woman,
a name you earned
if your lips were fishing lines,
your hair the color of tin,
if every evening you rocked
waiting for his sour breath,
if as every hour was struck
you rocked harder
keeping one eye on the Bible and humming
if anyone entered the room—

if every night you prayed
for the cops and ambulance to come keening,
Agony and Pestilence
riding the sirens.

THE FERRY

Whenever we needed to cross the Arkansas,
we had to take the dirt road to the ferry.
My father would drive.
My mother would fret
about missing the on-ramp,
driving off the other end,
getting caught by the dark.

After we bumped ourselves on
with a few other cars,
after the ferry coughed us away from shore,
the operator would shut the motor off
to drift as long as he dared.
Then we'd hear the motor again,
arguing with the current.

Thus we kept our course—
the river suffering us,
the sun easing down,
darkness closing over us
merciless as water.

SMOKE

Every year in the fall of the year
the hoboes, the same ones, came
scrabbling out of dusty nowhere
to harvest rice on my father's farm.

Then, in the fall that I turned sixteen,
my father changed to machines to farm with.
We never saw the hoboes again.
I remember one: a lanky artist

who shyly one day sketched for me
his idea of home. In hesitant charcoal
a roof took shape, a door, a chimney,
tieback curtains, a curl of smoke.

I imagined the kitchen's sunny cat,
the kettle, the stove, the bowl of flowers.
The person who knew to draw me that
was what I had been wanting. But how

could I have known— disdainful, already turned,
dancing toward Joey Hawkins down the road.

KISSING

One scene from my childhood:
Spending the night at my Aunt Eva's,
I have come downstairs at midnight
for a glass of milk.
She and her husband, Ferdinand,
sit at the kitchen table, their backs to me.
His left trouser leg
is rolled up to his thigh.
The stump of the leg he lost under a tractor
is propped on a stool,
gleaming in the lamplight.
My aunt and uncle bend above it,
laughing uncontrollably and kissing.

GOING BACK

My father's fields lie empty.
My mother's crape myrtles
have died in their sleep.
Daring the abandoned steps,
I enter the farmhouse
and my old room.

Summer evenings,
I used to open these windows
to the sound of a mockingbird,
the moon creaking up
like a stage set.

In the silence
a wasp bumps its way
along the ceiling.

TIES

It's late.
The mice in the walls have begun again.
The crickets have thinned
to a readable noise.
You look up from leafing a magazine
and say something woven out of our years together,
something only the two of us
would find amusing.
I think of this moment
as an incredible moth.
I want to keep it.

HAVING JUST MET

They slip away from the party.
He touches her arm, finding a memory there.
A train begins its noise across Missouri.
She brushes a thread from his sleeve.

THREADS

She had lost her memory at 35.
"So what?" her husband always says, and smiles
when someone remarks. Tonight they've come
to hear B.B. King in concert, live, in Memphis.
They saw B.B. last year, but she can't recall.
Her husband reminds her of that evening now,
quickly moving them through the smoky crowd
so she can get a closer look. In perfect
patience and love, he seats her where she commands
a clear view of the stage, closing his hand
and opening it on the smooth back of her chair.
At the small table, their elbows touch.
On the stage, B.B. is resplendent in black
and baby blue. The husband asks his wife
if she remembers the color of the jacket
when they saw him last. "Pink," she says.
It was orange. But he likes the way she touches his arm
when memory skims the surface of her mind
like, he imagines, the shadow of a gull
over sleeping water. His face burns
with the thought, the hope, that tonight in bed—
perhaps early, perhaps late—she will turn
to him and speak against his back, recalling
the jacket perfectly.

LOVE STORY

She confesses her love
for a man with a bald spot.
In summer the sun plays a one-note fortissimo upon it.
In winter it ices over.
She scatters suet on it.
Grackles sweep down.
She puts up a scarecrow for it
and a little canopy against the sleet.
Then they strut down the sidewalk together
like sleek, oiled crows.

What panoply! What noise!
The grackles clattering on the bald spot,
the magpies circling for the glint.

It's October now. First signs of sleet.
She tells him what she wants:
She wants to become a grackle,
beak and foot.

AT DUSK

A woman stands behind a farmhouse
in Kansas.
Soothing her skirt,
the woman leans into the wind.
The wind takes
some of the zinnias
out of the pocket of the skirt.

A man walks toward her,
coming in from the fields.
Distance dances around them
like sheets of dust.

IN PASSING

When they were married.
Listen, he said.
I've made a deal.
We're moving to Greece.
Ah, she said. Well.

When the child was born.
Listen, he said.
We'll name him Peele.
After my niece.
Well, she said. Ah.

When the child went to school.
Listen, he said.
He's learned to steal.
They've called the police.
Ah, she said. Well.

When the child married.
Listen, he said.
The baby's due.
The baby's dead.
Well, she said. Ah.

When she left him.
Listen, she said.
There's milk in the fridge,
and figs and bread.
Also a stew.
Listen, he said.
Please.

SHE RETURNS TO REMIND HIM HOW IT WAS WHEN IT WAS GOOD BETWEEN THEM

She has powers. She doesn't use a door.
She enters like smoke,
like sunlight through a cat's ear.

He looks up.
"I never wanted to see you again. Ever."
Still, when she inclines her head like that....
Something he says makes her laugh.
He feels clever.
"Well," he says. "We'll see."

COURTLY LOVE

A woman walks along Teche Bayou
with a man she loves.
A warm May evening.
He brings back for her a world
where her father wore a felt fedora
every day to work,
where her mother changed into a fresh dress
each afternoon.

The man touches her elbow.
Overhead, mimosas steep themselves
in bloom.

THE BREAKUP

It's likely that the cause of it
wasn't any one thing,
certainly not anything
either of them would believe.
Just the wearing away,
water constantly reminding stone.

AT THE AZURE SKY MOTEL

Slowly, checking his tie in the mirror,
he says what he is almost sure
will end it.
His words taste to her like the dust she recalls
from the seats of her grandfather's
second-hand Buick.

Trying to remember
where she left her car,
she walks by the pool.
The voices of children
fly at her like birds,
sassy and useless.

AFTER SUPPER

She liked the anger in her husband's eyes,
the moment of danger as she hurled the vase.
The vase fell childlike, fragile as prayer
or dusk as it waits to enter the tall grass.
Then the noise, bright and upright as pain.
When her husband spoke into the silence
the way he always did, she knew her lines.

A SECOND CUP OF COFFEE

According to their custom, Sundays,
a husband and wife exchanged the classifieds
and front page.
Pouring their second cups of coffee,
she told him she'd found out about the woman.
She placed and replaced her cup in the ring
it had made on the table.

They talked until the woman
became a name,
until how it began, and when,
advanced to a day and a street.

After she left,
taking the children with her,
he walked through rooms
not noticing,
forgetting where he had left his drink.

At dusk
he watched the mailbox,
the jonquils, the neighbor's elm
fall to the dark.
Only the white-blooming dogwood held
against it awhile.

ESTATE

They are talking in bed, late,
about their scheduled flight to the Bahamas.
Quietly, he says he guesses they ought to think about
their wills.

The way he says it, she thinks,
he might be suggesting they clean the basement.
What he proposes,
beneficiaries, executor,
a trust,
is logical, she guesses,
and sounds fair for the children.

On the radio someone is singing
"I've Got a Gal in Kalamazoo, Zoo, Zoo,"
a song they both remember from before the war.
Through the curtains comes a flicker of light,
someone turning into a driveway.
Her husband is suddenly asleep.
She tries to imagine.

IV

THE GOOD HAND

After a stroke of luck, my son's left hand
and arm lie lifeless. He has to remind
them, wherever he goes, to come along.
With the good hand he gives his old, strong

handshake, pulls on his shoes, adjusts his braces,
cooks, turns pages, touches the bored faces
of three dogs, struggles with rubber bands,
writes checks, drives a tractor, harrows and plants.

He caresses the hair of his two boys and his wife
and often takes with his good hand, my hand
or touches my shoulder when I sigh or laugh
over some loss we both can understand.

EVENING

From a wood beyond the fields,
something dark has not yet advanced
toward the yellow light
of the kitchen.
A woman puts away dishes.
A man goes through the mail.
A child leans over the table,
saying her homework.

The dog looks up once and growls
as if not meaning to, a sound
almost inaudible.
He clicks across the floor, nosing for crumbs.

IN THE OFFICE OF A LEADING ONCOLOGIST

The potpourri can't overcome
the dread smell rising in this room.
Here, the spunky, inseparable twins,
diagnosis and prognosis, grin
to escort the hapless to their graves.
Thin as a prisoner, one waves
absently. Some sleep. One,
bald as a cricket, squints in the sun.

As if a book, chapter and verse
fell open, I see: the Angel with spurs
like knives in her wings waits here.
Here is the abyss. What else shall I fear?
There is no balm in Gilead, nor slumber.
No Rose of Sharon. No sainted number.

Truth is freedom but the noose is tightening.
The nurse calls my name. I stand, frightened.

DOVES

At first he thought little of it,
two doves on a ledge
under the window
of his wife's hospital room,
their movements as fluid as iridescence,
as he waited with the kin
he'd called to come.

Later,
he saw that one of the doves was gone.
The one that was left
was lusterless and still as stone.
Ridiculous, he thought,
hugging himself,
to see that as a sign.

TAKING CHEMOTHERAPY

As it drips,
she thinks of herself
beside a trucker,
howling down an interstate.
Or fast dancing,
highest heels and briefest skirt,
her hair feathering against his cheek.

But that's one of her other selves,
the one who comes now
to sit beside her
and prattle about such things.

WAITING ROOM

I see you here most every day. How are you?
The coffee's gone. I've asked the desk for more
but I guess they're overworked and underpaid.
The nurses try. They've sure been good to us.
Who do you have here? I'm so sorry.
He's young, your son, isn't he, for that to happen?
Our son's here, too. He's not doing good. It's AIDS.
That was my husband that just left. He hates
for me to talk to anyone about Tommy.

Lord, it's expensive, having somebody here.
We're staying in our son's trailer. I'm afraid
he'll never go back to it. He's failed a lot
these last few days. How's your son? Well.
I'm so sorry. I'll be praying for him.

We live two hundred miles away. The driving
back and forth, we can't afford it. But even
staying in the trailer, you've got to eat,
and groceries are out of sight. We're getting too old
to drive in traffic. My husband doesn't do good
in places like this— the waiting, you know. Of course
you do. Does your son have children? Well,
there's no explaining these things. We take what comes.

I'm just thankful we can be here with Tommy.
You can't just walk away. Some do, you know.
Some of our friends said we ought to put
our son right out in the street. They would. My husband's

taking this real hard. He's aged ten years.
We've gone through nearly all our savings. I'm sure
you've noticed I'm missing some front teeth. Now,
I guess, I'll never get my partial plate.

I wish I could go buy me a new dress.
Might cheer Tommy up. He takes it hard
when I leave. All we can do is be here.
You can't just walk away. Remember, hon,
we're all right where we're supposed to be.
That's what I tell my husband. Here he is.

Herschel, come and meet someone. Her son
is in here, too. I simply can't believe
that traffic. I've lived my whole life in this state
and never been, not once, in this city.
We had our boy late, a good baby,
never any trouble at all. You have to go?

God bless. One day at a time, that's what I say.
Will you be here tomorrow? If there's a miracle,
we'll have hot coffee. But I wouldn't hold my breath.

HOW TO IMAGINE HOW IT WILL BE WHEN
THE DOCTOR COMES OUT TO SAY

Think of a man in Holland
the moment he sees a first break in the dike.
Think of Anne Frank at the moment she recognizes
the sound on the stair.

IN NO TIME

He follows the doctor out of his father's room.
"Without treatment, he'll be gone
in no time."
"With treatment?"
"A few months, maybe. It's hard to tell."
He thanks the doctor and says the family
will talk.

Taking the elevator down, he tries to remember
everything the doctor said.

Crossing the parking lot,
he hears a high and shifting V of geese.
He turns up his collar.

IN A NECK OF THE WOODS

(for John Downey)

The woods are dense in the remote county
where a man has disappeared.
Despite a desperate search,
there is no trace.
His wife told authorities
her husband left, alone,
to camp overnight.
She said he was dressed, as always,
in black from head to foot.

Perhaps, after dark and before the moon rose,
the man went for firewood.
Perhaps, falling in step beside him,
night assumed the man's shape,
easing perfectly
into his shoes.

GRACE

Seeing my grandchildren,
taking them in my arms,
I sometimes think it possible
to dance before the throne of God,
make small talk with Him,
my every jot and tittle of sin
forgiven.

CANCER

It eased under the door
like a mouse.
We scarcely noticed.
Then the scuttling.
Then the high squeak
that shattered the house.

INHERITANCE

A man dies,
leaving a farm and the house they grew up in
to his children,
who have married and moved away.
Indian summer brittles the fields.
Snow falls in the orchard.
The fields, the house, the tractor
shimmer and fade.

The children hire a lawyer
to settle everything.
Behind the windows of the house,
darkness and dust.

AT SUMMER'S END

A man calls his dog
at two a.m.
He whistles casually, as if to say
It's just a dumb dog.

The moon, a spider,
lets itself slowly down.

The man thinks of autumn.
He whistles again.

V

TEMPTING THE MUSE

Tilt your head provocatively,
round your vowels,
make a place for him
in the cleavage of your breasts.
Hope for the best.
What you'll get is anybody's guess.

Once, I pulled out all the stops
and a pickpocket wandered in,
reeking of booze and need;
and once, Death,
who apologized for getting the wrong house
and went on his way—
but not before his eyes,
red as a red snapper's,
undid every button of my dress.

WHO COULD ASK FOR ANYTHING MORE

Every Saturday
somebody in a cat costume
stands in the parking lot
across from my apartment,
hustling for the Mew-Mew Groom and Board.

His white fur needs a bath. One ear
is wrong.
There's a hole in his paw.

Although he dutifully waves to all who pass,
I have never seen anyone
wave back.
Or stop to leave a cat.

Staring out the window,
I picture the two of us together.
I know his hands and his face.
Yesterday we raked leaves.
Today, maybe we'll make
a pot of soup.

INTERSECTION

I set up my ironing board at an intersection
so as not to impede traffic.
I sprinkled a shirt to slight dampness,
rolled it into a ball
and waited hours,
as my mother had taught me.

Just as every thread was moist
but before mildew attacked,
I spread the shirt, damp and inviting,
on the board.

A musty steam arose
as the point of my iron touched the collar.

A man stopped his car to chat,
honking his horn.
Many interested people
leaned out of their cars.

ON THE BRINK

(for Tony Beasley)

A boy, a week away
from graduating high school,
is taken to dinner
by his father's oldest friend.
The brandies cleared,
the man removes from the cuffs of his shirt
a pair of 18 karat, ruby-studded cuff links
the boy has long admired.
He hands them to the boy
who tonight, for the first time,
confronts the stench
of circumstance and good luck.

THE PHENOMENOLOGICAL WORLD

As I drive by my neighbor's yard,
a swan I've mistaken daily for an ornament
raises a wing.

GRATITUDE

Sometimes it's a species of titmouse,
a wart hog,
a parrot who fancies himself a dandy,
can change your life.

A man in Ohio lost his wife
because a parrot they'd bought in Tahiti
slipped his cage.
The parrot's name was Starley.
The cage was papered in white snake.

When the parrot left, the wife left.
"Life without Starley," she said, "is a bubbleless champagne."

The man sold the Rolls and the houses.
He moved into the cage.
There he writes his autobiography,
which will come out in the spring
and contains a dedication to the parrot
who, rumor has it, keeps a house and a boy
in Deauville.
The dedication reads
"To Starley. Who made it all possible.
With eternal gratitude, Bill."

ACROSS TOWN

A woman spends the morning in juvenile court
with her son.
She sees him handcuffed and taken.
She goes home to a stifling house,
no trees in the yard.

Across town
under giant elms,
to the mild disinterest of the family cat,
a boy the same age as the woman's son
is lazily catching lizards.

PRIVILEGE

I see them in Wal-Mart.
She is a round-faced madonna,
a little on the beefy side
but sweet-faced, reminding me of days in June,
and crickets and water over stones.
He is bearded, going a trifle bald,
his face too large for the body
which has shrunk away.
His arms and legs
dangle like a rag doll's
as she carries him on his back in her arms.
Amazed, wondering what awful disease,
everyone stares.

A younger woman,
her hair falling from several crooked parts
like onion sets, strolls beside them.
The two children she offers up to Santa
howl as if they had been struck.
The group heads for Toys through Housewares,
the man and madonna smiling at each other
as she strokes his knee.

Walking to my car, I take out my wallet
to touch the snapshots
under the milky plastic.
My dead mother squints at me,
twisting her rings. My son,
splendid in tie and suit,
stands against solid mahogany.

THE ORDER OF THINGS

I tell a grandchild young enough
to care about it
how I discovered a chipmunk one afternoon
in a nearby field.
It was so well camouflaged, I said,
that I almost didn't see it.
What made you see it?
It moved.
Why did it move?
To find something to eat.
Then I told him about the hawk.

MERCY

The night after his two children burned
in a frame house in a searing drought,
the man, the neighbors said,
wandered through his yard
murmuring "Lord have mercy."
And the Lord sent rain.

LUCK

In the middle of phoning in an order
to Spiegel,
a woman discovers
she's been struck dumb.
When the doctors tell her there is no cure,
she smiles. If she could, she would tell them
her joy.
She remembers a time when she was a child,
pinning towels on the line
in the white and sparkling silence of
the farm.

THE NIGHT CLERK AT L. L. BEAN

(for Huey Crisp)

His phone rings almost all night,
as measured and intense
as somebody smoking a cigarette.
Taking an order for a monogrammed dog bed,
he remembers the time
a fox watched him, motionless,
from the edge of a field.

This is sometimes how grace comes to us,
sharp and fleeting as a paper cut.

HOLES

A woman showed her dry cleaner
the minute holes in a wool suit.
"When do they hatch?" she demanded.
"These moths lay their eggs, they hatch,
and what is hatched
eats holes in my good wool.
When? What time of year?"
She riveted her voice
into the eyes of the man who owned
O.K. and Milady Dry Cleaners.

The man looked down, folding the suit
like a pair of socks.
He told her to come back Friday.

The woman leaned over the counter.
"You don't know the first thing
about moths."

Until she died,
the woman spent one night a week
burning holes in her jackets and skirts,
burning the baby merino, the cashmere, alpaca,
gabardine, the serge.

She liked the fear on the man's face
when she came into his shop each Friday
with an armload of clothes.

SCORCH

After a summer flood
consumed the 40 acres of soybeans
and all but the roof of her house,
the woman who lived there
went back. The trees around the fields
were marked by a line so even
it might have been computer-drawn.
Above the line, the trees were green;
below it, brown without nuance.
Where the water and dirt had lingered
above the topmost windows,
the white two-storied house bore
a band as dirty as scorch.

Seeing that, the woman's breasts ached
as if she had lost a child.
She ordered scaffolding built,
and a catwalk to surround the house.
One night, climbing on the catwalk,
touching the house,
she felt the breath of what had been there—
vases and raincoats and dogs and shoes.

She knew what she must do.
Addressing the band that shone in the moonlight,
she walked the circumference of the house,
licking it clean.

WHAT WE NEED

It is just as well we do not see,
in the shadows behind the hasty tent
of the Allen Brothers Greatest Show,
Lola the Lion Tamer and the Great Valdini
in Nikes and jeans
sharing a tired cigarette
before she girds her wrists with glistening amulets
and snaps the tigers into rage,
before he adjusts the glimmering cummerbund
and makes from air
the white and trembling doves, the pair.